Praise For Gabriel Fitzmaurice

The best contemporary, traditional, popular poet in English.
RAY OLSON, *BOOKLIST*

Fitzmaurice is one of Ireland's leading poets ... a master of his art.
BOOKS IRELAND

Fitzmaurice is a wonderful poet.
GILES FODEN, *THE GUARDIAN*

The people's poet.
BILLY KEANE, *THE IRISH INDEPENDENT*

Fitzmaurice's signature rhymes are clear and true ... [he] expresses grief, joy, faith and doubt, his poems proof that the universal shows itself most clearly in ... concentrated particularities.
MARTINA EVANS, *THE IRISH TIMES*

Ireland, particularly the South ... finds its local bard in Gabriel Fitzmaurice ... thereby making such 'singing' socially responsible in a way Wordsworth would have endorsed.
FRANCIS O'HARE, HU, *THE HONEST ULSTERMAN*

[T]he poetry of Gabriel Fitzmaurice is salutary ... This is poetry of the felt experience as D.H. Lawrence would have

advocated ... Fitzmaurice's elevation of Moyvane has resonances with Oliver Goldsmith's Auburn, and Patrick Kavanagh's Shancoduff. The eternal verities of place, character, and local colour are frozen like a Vermeer ... Gabriel Fitzmaurice's poetry is visionary and durable, unforced and deceptively simple.
BRENDAN HAMILL, *FORTNIGHT*

Not unlike those of Goldsmith and Burns, these poems are endowed with charm, wit and generosity of spirit ... He transcends sentimentality to effect what that redoubtable school inspector Matthew Arnold would recognise as 'a criticism of life'.
JAMES J. MCAULEY, *THE IRISH TIMES*

Real stories told in real language, the poems of Gabriel Fitzmaurice have the simple reality and powerful magic of the true folk song ... and the songs are haunting and beautiful.
KRIS KRISTOFFERSON

THE BEST-LOVED POEMS
OF
GABRIEL FITZMAURICE

*Introduction by
Declan Kiberd*

MERCIER PRESS

MERCIER PRESS
Cork
www.mercierpress.ie

© Gabriel Fitzmaurice, 2024

Introduction © Declan Kiberd

ISBN: 978-1-78117-944-4

978-1-78117-945-1 E Book

Cover art: Brenda Fitzmaurice 'Lighthouses'
Author photograph: Tom Fitzgerald
Cover design: Sarah O'Flaherty

This book is sold subject to the condition that it shall not, by way of trade or otherwise, be lent, resold, hired out or otherwise circulated without the publisher's prior consent in any form of binding or cover other than that in which it is published and without a similar condition including this condition being imposed on the subsequent purchaser.

No part of this publication may be reproduced or transmitted in any form or by any means, electronic or mechanical, including photocopying, recording or any information or retrieval system, without the prior permission of the publisher in writing.

For my dear friend Győző Ferencz

Poet and Professor

Contents

Introduction	9
A Middle-Aged Orpheus Looks Back at his Life	15
To My D-28	16
In Memory of My Mother	18
I Sing of Michael Hartnett	19
So What If there's No Happy Ending?	20
Death of a Playwright	21
Dad	22
My Best Friend	23
The Woman of the House	26
Big Con	30
Lassie	40
Ruckard Drury	41
His Last Pint	43
The Day Christ came to Moyvane	44
Before the Word 'Fuck' came to Common Use	45
Help Me make it through the Night	46
On Hearing Johnny Cash's American Recordings	48
Homage to Thomas MacGreevy	49
'I Thirst'	50
The Díseart	52
Knockanure Church	54
When I Pray	55
When I Die	56

In the Woods	58
The Road to Damascus	59
The Hurt Bird	60
A Boy I Know	67
I'm Proud to be Me	69
Dan Breen	70
The Mother	71
Galvin and Vicars	72
Munster Football Final 1924	74
Ireland Takes Her Place among the Nations of the Earth	75
A Parent's Love	76
Grá Tuismitheora	77
To My Son as He Leaves Home	78
To My Daughter, Pregnant	79
Nanas	80
Sonnet to Brenda	81
Just to be Beside You is Enough	82
Old Lovers	83
Reading William Wordsworth	84
Drinking in the Square	85
Acknowledgements	86
Biographical Note	87

Introduction

If all art aspires to the condition of music, then poetry has a double advantage over, say, painting or even sonata. For it can combine melody with direct utterance, song and words. This is of course a risky coupling, for sometimes the sounds may not equal the music in quality or the music may chime with an over-obviousness that betrays the language. Not so in the case of Gabriel Fitzmaurice, whose work often seems to return us to earlier centuries, when English poets sang to the accompaniment of a lute or Gaelic bards employed the services of a *reacaire* plucking a stringed instrument.

It's little short of a scandal that words and instrumental music got separated in the intervening centuries, amid the growing specialisation of roles that characterise modernity. Even those songs which still are accompanied by instruments often declined into banality, leaving the music to do the main work (consider the tinkling lyrics of Eoghan Rua Ó Súilleabháin or the facile pop music of Pat Boone).

Gabriel Fitzmaurice has never fallen into these traps. His poems are examples of an archaic avant-garde, at once very traditional and strikingly contemporary; yet their music and words consort in ways which are scarcely ever practised now. He often employs rhyme in the predictable forms, yet the sound of the clinching second word turns out to seem at once inevitable yet utterly surprising – rather as we find in the concluding moments of a classic play. In this he has something in common with Keats, who held that poetry should take us off our guard by words of surprisingly 'fine excess'. Like Keats, too, he has managed to introduce conversational rhythms into even the strictest balladic metres – relaxation and rigour in one. He has the studied fastidiousness of Renaissance sonneteers but expressed with an urgent lucidity of that language spoken every day in the streets.

This is found at its most lyrical in those poems written as sonnets, a form once reserved for aristocratic subjects but here devoted to such everyday themes as a daughter collecting new-laid eggs, or a celebration of the rudimentary architecture of Knockanure church (a *teach an phobail* if ever there was one), or a lovely lyrical rewrite in demotic of Shakespeare's 'Shall I Compare Thee?'(surely one of the most moving celebrations of the mature, late years of a loving marriage written in our time).

These words all display a fine reverence for the exacting sonnet form, but here is a poet unafraid to mingle some witty insolence with a considerable reverence. The recent lyrics devoted to Wordsworth at the collection's end can seem downright cheeky ('Reading Wordsworth'), even to the point of savage parody ('Oh, joy, that in our embers ...'), as if a student once compelled to learn these rather vicar-like lines can at last take a merry revenge. This would be true of the companion-piece which takes 'Westminster Bridge' – 'Earth hath not anything to show more fair' – but one can't help sensing also an undertow of homage, imitation being an ultimate flattery. After all, Wordsworth's poem was really a study of *rus in urbe*, of the village-like feel of London at dawn – 'smokeless air', 'calm so deep' – of exactly the sort at which Fitzmaurice excels (his own descriptions of dawn and dusk are comparable to the magnificent 'Waterloo Sunset' by the Kinks). And, though seemingly derided here, 'Oh, joy, that in our embers' may be the lead-in to lines which are saying precisely the same thing as this poet: that older age, though not for wimps, is definitely something to be celebrated. In some of the finest verses here, as I have implied, mature married love has at last found a laureate, after all those Renaissance and Romantic songs and sonnets devoted to youthful early crushes.

The technical gifts Fitzmaurice displays are practised in a clear, lucid, even stripped-back idiom, quite at variance with the 'poetic diction' which so irritated Wordsworth and Coleridge. They produced their 'lyrical ballads' in open defiance of it. Fitzmaurice understands that unless you are a genius – and especially if you're a genius – it is better to be comprehensible. This stripped-down word-music is rightly saluted in the ballads of Johnny Cash ('to pare life back to where things don't deceive'). It is based, in my view, on Emerson's very American observation that we must be sensitive to the total meaning of every word, because every word (even the now casually-abused 'fuck') was once a poem.

Every art-work is possible only to one person at one time and in one place; and Fitzmaurice remains always true to the colour of his own locality: Moyvane, Knockanure, Listowel. (He can be over-critical of it – surely the passing of John B. Keane, though greatly to be regretted, did not mean that there were no writers left in Listowel, though this may be the sort of poetic license employed in the *marbhna* by Gaelic poets!). Fitzmaurice writes very feelingly of his parents, wife, children – and of the local children whom he taught for years (how astute he is in noticing that the sounds of hilarity and melancholy from kids can at strange moments seem so alike). He identifies the instincts of animals, from loyal dogs to hurt birds, as they engage in a wordless communication with this lyricist. The celebration of drinking, which in earlier work linked him to *spailpín* poets, has taken on a darker hue by now, as it is conducted in proximity to the encroaching death of friends, or even to Jesus on the Cross ('I Thirst'). Which inevitably brings him to poems saluting Michael Hartnett, arguably the most under-rated Irish poet of his generation, and to Thomas MacGreevy, a Catholic modernist of a previous dispensation. This poet, like MacGreevy and the stained-glass artist Harry Clarke, practises a religious belief which is sorely tested by the rigidities of old-style Catholic rule-keeping, but which somehow survives these indignities while reporting them with clarity, because his faith is in the spirit and in the other-world, not in the dirigiste puritans who reduced religious practice from a relationship with God to a matter of social decorum. The actor, Peter O'Toole, captured the interiority of true spirituality in the same way as Fitzmaurice, who seems to quote Mother Teresa who once said 'I talk/ He doesn't listen'. In his great film *The Ruling Class*, O'Toole plays a character who claims to be God and, when asked how this could possibly be, he explains 'because every time I pray I have the feeling that I'm talking to myself'.

There is much wisdom alongside the music of these lyrics. The hurt bird cannot be morally improved by pain endured, which in turn implies a deep question as to the character-forming nature (if any) of actual human suffering. The schoolchildren who look in amazement at the wounded bird are a reminder that teachers must always learn to see the world through their eyes: 'Who would become a teacher/Must first become a child'. (The problem, as Wilde mischievously observed, is that in most cases it is those who have forgotten how to learn who have taken to teaching).

The advice to a departing son certainly improves vastly upon that given to Laertes by Polonius. And the openness of this writer to both sides in the War of Independence indicates what John Hume once said was badly needed – 'a well-balanced Irish person with a chip on each shoulder'. The role of sport in reconciling belligerents of the Civil War is far too seldom recognised as in a fine sonnet here: but it gives the lie to George Orwell's silly observation that sport is nothing more than war by other means. And the final openness to inward migration suggests that the time may have at last come to write Emmet's epitaph, in a poem which recalls Heaney's 'inner émigré, grown long-haired and thoughtful'.

Devotees of Fitzmaurice's superb children's poetry (I'm an admirer of Ireland's A.A. Milne myself) may be sorry not to see more included here, but, vitally, the poems he has included capture the questions, voices and experiences of children. The child is indeed father of the man; and here the mature man has his eloquent and terse say.

DECLAN KIBERD

A Middle-Aged Orpheus Looks Back at his Life

For Kris & Lisa Kristofferson

I took my voice to places where no man
Should take his voice and hope that it would sing.
All I wanted when I began
Was to strike up my guitar and do my thing.
Haunted from home, I sang my song
While all around forgot their words and fell;
In the underworld I blundered on
In regions where not it, but I, was hell.

I took my voice to places where no man
Should take his voice and hope that it would sing;
I paid the price in lines that rhyme and scan,
The last illusion to which singers cling
Before they yield their song up to the truth
They thought they could outsing in foolish youth.

To My D-28

Your body's unblemished
And sweetly you're strung,
A beauty I dreamed of
Since I was young,
But I'm middle aged
Losing hair, overweight,
And it's now you come to me,
My D-28.

As youngsters we dreamed
And talked of guitars,
We played out our crushes
On prized Yamahas,
And though we made music
When out on a date,
We wished we were playing
A D-28.

We played Epiphones, Yamahas,
Fenders - all good;
We played on them music
To suit every mood,
But deep down we dreamed
That sooner or late

We'd all find our very own
D-28.

The past becomes present,
The dream becomes true.
It was music I loved, dear,
(I thought it was you);
You're all that I dreamed of
But now it's too late
For I'm pledged to another,
My D-28.

And still we make music
But now we both know
That there's no going back
To the long, long ago
For my road is taken,
I'm resigned to my fate,
My first and forever
D-28.

D-28: A Martin guitar

In Memory of My Mother

My mother lived for books though nearly blind.
An invalid, she read while she could see.
The only pleasure left her was her mind.

The books she read that pleased her were designed
To strip her life down to a clarity.
My mother lived for books though nearly blind

While I'd read all the comics I could find;
Confined to bed, she'd read 'good books' to me.
The only pleasure left her was her mind.

Delighting in the vision of her kind,
That second sight, the gift of poetry,
My mother lived for books though nearly blind,

Books I read from bookshelves that were lined
With poems she'd recite from memory.
The only pleasure left her was her mind.

And I remembered as I launched and signed
The first slim *Poems* of my maturity
How Mammy lived for books though nearly blind,
The only pleasure left to her, her mind.

I Sing of Michael Hartnett

Ruthless with a biro,
Crossing out what you
Considered unbecoming
To the beautiful and true

In my poems, your pupil,
You taught me all you knew
Over pints of porter.
In the end they did for you.

And when you died, your people
Laid you to rest
Among your friends and neighbours
In your beloved Newcastlewest

Where poets flocked to bid farewell
To the little poet-bird
Silent now forever
Word, by word, by word.

I sing of Michael Hartnett
Who bore the poet's cross
All the way to Calvary.
We're the poorer for his loss.

So What If there's No Happy Ending?

In memoriam Michael Hartnett

So what if there's no happy ending?
Don't be afraid of the dark;
Open the door into darkness
And hear the black dogs bark.

Oh what a wonder is darkness!
In it you can view
The moon and stars of your nature
That daylight hid from you.

Open the door into darkness,
There's nothing at all to fear -
Just the black dogs barking, barking
As the moon and stars appear.

Death of a Playwright

In memoriam John B. Keane

'John B. is dead', Listowel said
Incomprehension on its brow;
'John B. is dead', Listowel said,
'We're only an ordinary town now'.

Dad

A man before his time, he cooked and sewed,
Took care of me - and Mammy in her bed,
Stayed in by night and never hit the road.
I remember well the morning she was dead
(I'd been living up in Arklow - my first job,
I hit the road in patches coming home),
He came down from her room, began to sob
'Oh Gabriel, Gabriel, Gabriel, Mam is gone'.
He held me and I told him not to cry
(I loved her too, but thought this not the place -
I went up to her room, cried softly 'Why?'
Then touched her head quite stiffly, no embrace).
Now when the New Man poses with his kid,
I think of all the things my father did.

My Best Friend

My best friend was Grandad.
I used to stay at his house on Friday nights
And that was great fun.
He used to take me to the chipper
After the nine o'clock news
And he'd buy two cartons of curried chips and two sausages
And we'd eat them in his kitchen during the *Late Late Show*.
He used to come up to our house on Sundays for dinner
And I'd always want to sit beside him at the table.

I remember one Christmas I had just got a snooker table.
Grandad came up for Christmas dinner
And I had asked everybody else to play with me.
They all said no, they were too busy.
Grandad was in the middle of setting the table
And I asked him to play and he said he would.
He came over
And I actually had to place the balls for him
It was so long since he had played snooker!

Well Grandad was my best friend;
He was so kind.
He was just unique to me.
Like he didn't know much Irish
Because when he was young he hadn't much time for school
(He had to help at home on the farm, he said,
And at fourteen years had to hire himself with farmers
Because he had thirteen brothers and sisters
And times were bad)
But I often did my Irish homework with him and he always ended up right.

I remember the day Grandad died.
It was March.
I can't remember the date.
He rang Mom and said he thought he was having a heart attack.
We rushed down to his house -
We got there in two and a half minutes
And when we went in we found Grandad lying on the floor moaning.
And then he just died.
And I was below in the room crying
And then Mom and Nessa and Dad started crying too.

At the Funeral Parlour I forgot myself
And said 'I'm sitting beside Grandad.'
But Grandad was in his coffin.
He was dead.

It was fine until they closed the coffin
And then I knew I'd never see him again in this
    life.

Goodbye, Grandad, my best friend.
Goodbye
Goodbye.

Adapted from a story written by my son John.

The Woman of the House

The village – Ballygariff
Sometime in the past
Where the clock advanced for Closing Time
Is the only thing that's fast.

In her pub, Maggie Browne
(Browne's her maiden name)
Serves pints and whiskies to a group
Who've recently come home

On holiday from England,
They wear their Sunday best -
They're out to prove that exile
Does better than the rest

Who stay at home in Bally
And work that windswept hill
And so they dress in Sunday best
And flash big twenty bills.

Enter then Tom Guiney,
The singer, for a beer;
He's bought tobacco for himself,
Sugar, tea and flour

For his wife above in Barna,
He comes in for 'just the one'
But the exiles stand him porter
And demand of him a song.

All afternoon he sings for them;
At "The Home I Left Behind"
The exiles back in Bally
Stare into black pints

For song is all that's left them
Of Bally long ago,
The past is all that's left them,
The only home they know.

Tom Guiney, man of honour,
Will stand his round
Though what's left in his pocket
Will hardly make a pound.

Nonetheless he calls for
A drink for the company -
'Twould never be said in Bally
He drank all day for free.

Maggie Browne sets up the drinks
And Tom must now admit

That he hasn't enough to pay for them –
Could she put it on the slate?

She does. And on with singing
But Maggie bides her time
And in a private moment
Takes Tom aside.

'Tom,' she says, 'You'll never
Call for a drink again
With no money in your pocket
For a crowd like them.

'Call for your drink, Tom Guiney,
And when I put it up
If you've no money in your pocket
Let them take a sup

'Or two and let them talk
And then come up to me
And ask me for the change
Of the fiver you gave me;

'And Guiney, boy, you'll get it –
Never, never again
Let on that you've no money
To a crowd like them'.

The village – Ballygariff.
Time – the present. Now
We come to bury Maggie Browne;
We take and drink our stout –

We do this in memory
Of a woman we well know,
Exalter of the humble
In a singer long ago.

Big Con

For my dear friend Con Greaney, singer

Big Con lives in the mountain
In a thatched house on his own,
His wife is dead fifteen years,
His family, long grown,

Have left the ancestral mountain
But Con will not remove:
His life is in the mountain,
His love.

Born on the mountain
These eighty years and more,
Not born so much as quarried;
The mountain life was poor

('Twas Rooska of the curlew),
But not poor of heart –
He came from singing people
Whose life was art.

Big Con, King of singers
Has songs that only he

Brought from the singing people.
He sang his songs for me.

      ***

Once upon an emptiness
The Lost Man came home -
The man was lost because
He had lost his song.

He searched everywhere but couldn't find it
(Did he ever have the song?
He wondered)
So he collected songs.

He went to the oldest singers,
He learned all their songs,
He sang them for his people
But still did not belong.

One night, he sang with Donie Lyons,
A farmer out of Glin,
A flute player and singer.
Donie said to him:

'There's an old man in the West Limerick Hills
That no one remembers now;
He might have what you're looking for'.
They finished their pints of stout;

They bought beer and whiskey
As an offering to Big Con
And drove into the mountain.
Would the giant sing his songs?

'Ye're welcome as the flowers of May',
Beamed Big Con, 'Come in!
How're you keeping, Donie?
How're ye all in Glin?'

'Fine, Con,' replied Donie;
'Con, I brought this man,
He's recorded many singers,
He's looking for a song.'
'If I have the song, he'll get it;
Make yereselves at home.'

We drank a few throws of whiskey,
Knocked back a couple of beers
Then Con exploded into song.
The Lost Man, startled, hears

Him bend the air and twist it –
An old life made anew,
And every time 'twas different
And every time 'twas true,
The song that he was looking for,

The self that he once knew.

***

We break for beer and whiskey
And then return to song,
And song turns to story:
The story is Big Con ...

'I remember my time in England,
Times were bad 'round here;
I had to leave my wife and children
In Rooska for a year.

'I took the boat for England,
Met my brother at the quay –
He brought me home to Huddersfield,
Looked for work for me.

'A few days I lived off him
And then one night he said
"There's a job going with the darkies –
I'd be careful of that crowd."

'But I worked away with the black men,
They were the same as me –
They found me strange, I found them strange;

We worked silently

'Until one day my partner
Forgot to bring his lunch –
He was leaving the job at dinner hour
For what you'd now call "brunch".

'"There's no need to go", I told him,
"I have plenty for us here";
I gave him half my sandwiches;
After work we went for beer.

'And here was I – someplace –
Black men all around;
They stood to me all evening,
Wouldn't let me stand a round.

'And what was it but a sandwich,
Pan loaf that made a friend?
They drove me home at Closing Time;
My brother was out of his mind:

'"Jeezus, I thought they'd killed you –
In that place at night;
You don't know where you're going".
'Them people is all right',

I told him.
'I'm welcome there, they said,
And the reason that I'm welcome
Is I gave a black man bread'.

And one day in the woollen mill,
A bale fell on my foot,
I was going to the doctor
But my partner said, 'No good! –

You no go to doctor,
Him take you off the job,
We do your work till you better,
You no lose a bob'.

'So I turned up each morning
And the black men did my work,
We went for beer each evening
And I'd go home after dark.

'And the night before I was leaving
I spent it with the blacks;
They were singing their songs
And one said in the jacks:

"'Big Con, you have your own songs?";
I told him I could sing

But they wouldn't know my singing;
Still, they made me sing.

'I sang the songs the mountain sang
At Feast and Fast and Fair
And d'you know, 'twas like the mountain
Had removed from here to there.

'We drank all night, we said goodbye,
We'd never meet again;
I took the boat next evening,
Went back to bogs and drains.'

***

At peace at last, the Lost Man
Sent Con's songs throughout the land
And the legend grew with the singers
Who sought out this old man …

'There's a Concert up in Dublin, Con;
Everyone will be there;
Will you come and sing your songs for us
Pure as mountain air?'

On the night of the big Concert,
His first time so far from home

Since he returned from Huddersfield,
We gazed around our room

(I'd travelled to Dublin with him –
He needed me, he said;
He didn't know Dublin
And I did).

A hotel room, en suite, TV,
But Con got bored with that,
He took off downstairs to find the bar
For a pint, a pipe and chat.

Who is this old singer
They're putting on tonight?
An old man from the mountains.
Can he do it here? He might ...

The MC shepherds Big Con
Backstage from the bar:
'Con,' he chides, 'this is no pub,
This stage is for stars –

'You can't just start up singing,
You must talk first to the crowd;
Do you think, Con, you can do it?'
Con just laughs out loud –

'I see the Pope in Galway
When he said Mass on the TV –
He told the crowd he loved them;
Don't worry about me.'

'Ladies and gentlemen, Big Con'
Silence, a polite clap,
And Con saunters out on stage
With his pint and cap.

He remembers the Pope in Galway
As he faces the dark Hall -
'People of Dublin, I loves ye!'
The whole place is enthralled;

He sings six songs, his quota,
But the crowd cries out for more,
And when he's finished singing,
They clap till their hands are sore

***

Big Con and the Lost Man
Travel home by train,
And the Lost Man says to Big Con,
'I won't see your like again.'

Over in the West Limerick Hills
In a thatched house with his dog,
Big Con lives, a giant.
If his life was one hard slog

Now they come throughout the land
To learn at his feet –
'Ye're welcome as the flowers of May'
I hear an old man greet.

Lassie

At ninety years he fell into a drain -
That's what John Bradley tells me from his bed
(Hospital plays tricks on old men's brains);
But for his dog, he tells me, he'd be dead.
How fact and fiction make us what we are –
He fell at home at bedtime in the dark
(The drain was years ago outside a bar);
His faithful dog had more sense than to bark –
She lay down on her master all night long,
Licked his face and wrapped him from the cold,
And when the ambulance came to take out John,
Lassie stayed and couldn't be consoled.
She guards his house and lets no stranger through -
When there's nothing left, love finds such things
    to do.

Ruckard Drury

Ruckard Drury, *spailpín*,
Laboured all his life
For pig-ignorant farmers.
One day, a farmer's wife

Had Drury at her table,
Her fare was tea and bread
But she served him up bad butter
Which Ruckard Drury fed

To a farm-cat at the table
And when the wife saw that,
She turned on the *spailpín*
Who replied: 'Do you see that cat?

'You gave me rotten butter;
You saw what he did, no doubt –
That cat there had to lick his arse
To take the taste from his mouth.

'That cat there had to lick his arse
The butter was so bad',
Then Drury left her table
And the daily bread it had.

Drury left her table
Hungry still, but proud;
A *spailpín*, he's remembered
Hungry but unbowed.

Ruckard Drury.

Ruckard Drury: Ruckard (Michael) Drury was born in the Bog Lane, Knockanure, in the parish of Moyvane in 1864 and died in 1952.
Spailpín*: (Irish) a migratory farm labourer*

His Last Pint

He came into the village one last time
Defying cancer by an act of will
As he came into the village in his prime.

He left with me as his clock began to chime
Nine o'clock; swallowing a pill,
He came into the village one last time.

We stopped at Kincaid's Bar; he couldn't climb
Out of my car until I helped him. Still,
As he came into the village in his prime,

He walked in unsupported, and I'm
Certain that the drinkers felt a chill
As he came into the village one last time.

He called for a Carlsberg and lime
Too weak now for the Guinness that he'd swill
When he came into the village in his prime.

But the cancer couldn't take his state of mind:
From the tap of life the dying drank his fill –
He came into the village one last time
As he came into the village in his prime.

The Day Christ came to Moyvane

He came to fix umbrellas,
Kettles, basins, pans;
The squad car turned in my yard
And jumped the traveller man –

'What are you doing?', 'What's your name?',
'Get going out of here';
The traveller man walked down the drive,
My dog snapped at his heels.

But the traveller man was used to dogs,
He just kept walking on,
And as he walked he whistled
And was gone.

The Guard was doing his duty –
There had been reports
Of travellers casing houses.
I'd been robbed before,

So I thanked the Guard and offered him
A beer, a cup of tea,
And as we talked, the traveller man
Walked farther away from me.

Before the Word 'Fuck' came to Common Use

Before the word 'fuck' came to common use
(Even toddlers going to play school know it now),
Before the lid was raised on child abuse,
We said that we were innocent. But how?
We heard the whispers and we went along
Protecting those who were above the law
In a world we eulogise ('knew right from wrong),
A world nostalgia paints without a flaw.
Before the word 'fuck' came to common use
We were children and our masters ran the show ...
Guilty as condemned, it's no excuse
To plead that in the past we didn't know.
Before the word 'fuck' came to common use
Children mattered less than their abusers.

Help Me make it through the Night

The old lady greets Kristofferson with
'You must listen to my story,
How you helped me make it through the night.

'I was a married woman with four children
And my Church decreed it wasn't right
To use contraceptives with my husband
So I'd scrub the floors at bedtime
Till my husband was asleep
And the only company I had,
The only help in my plight,
Was you singing over and over
"Help Me Make it through the Night".

'And how once I was in Saint Patrick's Purgatory,
A penitential island where I went
To walk barefoot, hungry, thirsty
That I might learn what my life meant
And in confession to the priest there
I opened, heart and soul,
And told him that we had four children,
That at nights I scrubbed the floors
Because the Church didn't allow contraceptives,

That, on my knees till my husband slept,
That only then would I cease scrubbing
And retire to our marriage bed.
I asked him to advise me
But he left me dead –
He couldn't help me and my husband
Was all he said.

So know when you sing that song again, Kris,
That I see it in this light –
A woman on her knees scrubbing.

You helped me make it through the night.'

On Hearing Johnny Cash's American Recordings

The great ones have the courage to believe,
The courage to go naked if so called,
To pare life back to where things don't deceive;
Let those ashamed of feeling be appalled,
These simple songs of love and death ring true
In an age when we're afraid to show the heart –
'Whatever you say, say nothing', this in lieu
Of a creed that years ago joined prayer and art.
We say nothing and mean nothing now that we
Lose belief and, cynics in our loss,
Look down on the believer, this poetry –
The gospel of a soul that takes its cross,
Songs a life has earned or else are trash,
Salvation, suffered, sung by Johnny Cash.

Homage to Thomas MacGreevy

MacGreevy, poet, Catholic, you found your place
In a world where art redeemed, the word was true,
In a creed that raised living into grace
As, a poet and a Catholic, I must too.
The life a Catholic has to face
Is no different to the life we all go through
Losing heart at the squalid commonplace
But for a vision that redeems its ugly hue.
So welcome, then, the hopeless and the base,
The depths descended as their artists drew
Their Christs amid dejection and disgrace,
Christ my muse in poem, in pub, in pew.
With MacGreevy, poet, Catholic, I find my place
In a creed that raises living into grace.

'I Thirst'

Midnight Mass one Christmas Eve,
The parish comes to pray –
A midnight of nostalgia
After a hard day;

For some have been preparing
Their Christmas at the sink,
And others have spent the day
Revelling in drink.

At Midnight Mass, the parish
Bows its head in prayer –
All but one have come along
In pious posture there.

All day, he's been drinking
In The Corner House;
When it comes to closing time
He buys, to carry out
For after Mass, two bottles
Of Guinness Extra Stout.

And he stands there with the others
At the back wall of the church;

When it comes to the offertory,
Suddenly with a lurch

He staggers up the centre aisle
While the crowd looks on in shock,
Halting at the altar rails,
Careful not to drop

The bottles, he takes them out,
Plants them on the rails,
Faces the congregation,
Waves and then repairs

To the back and anonymity,
Hitches up his arse,
And some are shocked, and some amused
At this unholy farce.

But the Christ who thirsts on Calvary
Has waited all these years
For a fellow cursed with the cross of thirst
To stand him these few beers.

The Díseart

A sign points to the Díseart,
A place of prayer and art –
An empty convent chapel
Whose private Harry Clarkes

(Twelve stained glass lancet windows)
Are public here today,
And some come here for beauty,
And some come here to pray.

Once I prayed in beauty
In the sanctuary of art –
How much was self deception?
What now is Harry Clarke?

What signifies the light
That's filtered in this place?
In this convent chapel
For some it still means grace.

But I leave the chapel,
It's given me no peace
(I'm through with self-deception),
Face the teeming streets.

Nothing was transfigured
But I saw things in his light,
A beauty not sufficient
To transform my plight.

And yet, the heavens streaming
Through windows stained to art
Illuminate the darkness
In the chapel of my heart.

Díseart: *(Irish) a retreat, a hermitage; a deserted place, a desert*
Harry Clarke (1889–1931) was Ireland's outstanding stained glass artist

Knockanure Church

For Fintan O'Toole

A place of worship, simple and austere;
'Sixties architecture past its date.
I wonder what it is that draws me here
To a building local people seem to hate.
The church of their affection, knocked, made way
For the 'garage on the hill' in its design –
Bare brick, flat roof, no steeple, here I pray.
The spirit of this building's kin to mine.

My God's a God who strips me in this place –
No cover here, the lines are stark and spare;
Through the years, I've grown into this space
Where work of human hands raised art to prayer,
The same the builders raised up once at Chartres
But plainer here, an answer to my heart.

When I Pray

I talk to myself,
The only person
I can't lie to.

Whether God is listening
Or not,
I don't know
But I talk
As if He were.

I talk,
He doesn't answer.
Not that I expect Him to.

But wisdom comes
Through talking
As if God were listening
Where only truth will do.

When I Die

Don't eulogise me with pious lies.

Tell them
I was a man of pubs,
A man of song,
But there were times
When even singing and drinking
Let me down;

Tell them
That I didn't believe enough
In myself or God,
That I didn't always live
As a good man should;

Tell them that I loved
But not enough,
Tell them that loving me
Was often rough;

Tell them I was selfish,
I was vain
But didn't diminish responsibility
Through pain;

Tell them I was no stranger to the dark
But was lit by stars
When the black dogs barked;

Tell them I was honest,
That I lied,
But remember to tell them also
That I tried.

Don't bury me with platitudes
About Christian death.

Say me like I was
And commit me to the earth.

In the Woods

X on a tree trunk
Marks no buried treasure here
Children wonder why.

***

A rotting tree stump
In the middle of the woods
Mushrooms with new life.

***

Where there are nettles
There are dock leaves to heal us
In a spot nearby.

The Road to Damascus

She looks me squarely in the eye
And says (no trace of fright),
'You think you're the biggest man in the world',
And, to my shame, she's right.

I persecute with learning,
Make her, and others, fail
In the name of education.
It's I, not she, who've failed.

This, then, is the moment,
Struck from my high horse,
I see the child before me –
Child most wondrous.

She looks at me, offended,
Her accusation mild.
Who would become a teacher
Must first become a child.

The Hurt Bird

After playtime
Huddled in the classroom ...

In the yard
Jackdaws peck the ice
While the class guesses
The black birds:

Blackbirds?
(Laughter).

Crows?
Well yes ...
But jackdaws.
Those are jackdaws.
Why do they peck the ice?

Wonder
Becomes jackdaws' eyes
Rummaging the ice

Till suddenly
At the window opposite

– Oh the bird!
The poor bird!
At the shout
The jackdaws fright.

Sir, a robin sir ...
He struck the window
And he fell
And now he's dying
With his legs up
On the ice:

The jackdaws
 Will attack it sir,

They will rip its puddings out.

I take the wounded bird,
Deadweight
In my open palm

– No flutter
No escaping

And lay it on the floor near heat,
The deadweight
Of the wound

Upon my coat.

Grasping
The ways of pain,
The pain of birds
They cannot name,
The class are curious
But quiet:

They will not frighten
The struggle
Of death and living.

Please sir,
Will he die?

And I
Cannot reply.

Alone
With utter pain

Eyes closed

The little body
Puffed and gasping

Lopsided
Yet upright:

He's alive,
The children whisper
Excited
As if witnessing
His birth.

Would he drink water sir?
Would he eat bread?
Should we feed him?

Lopsided
The hurt bird
With one eye open
To the world
Shits;

He moves
And stumbles.

I move
To the hurt bird:

The beak opens
– For food

Or fight?

I touch
The puffed red breast
With trepid finger;

I spoon water
To the throat:
It splutters.

Children crumb their lunches
Pleading to lay the broken bread
Within reach of the black head.

The bird
Too hurt to feed
Falls in the valley
Of the coat,
And as I help
It claws
And perches on my finger
Bridging the great divide
Of man and bird.

He hops
From my finger
To the floor

And flutters
Under tables
Under chairs

Till exhausted
He tucks his head
Between wing and breast
Private
Between coat and wall.
The class
Delights in silence
At the sleeping bird.

The bird sir ...
What is it –
A robin?
– Look at the red breast.

But you never see a robin
With a black head.

I tell them
It's a bullfinch
Explaining the colours why:

I answer their questions
From the library.

And the children draw the bullfinch

– With hurt
And gasp
And life

With the fearlessness of pain
Where the bird will fright

And in the children's pictures
Even black and grey
Are bright.

A Boy I Know

He rises every morning,
Gets up all alone,
No one up to wake him,
He does it on his own.

No one makes his breakfast,
They leave him cash instead
And he goes up to the local shop
To be fed.

A can of Coca-Cola,
A jumbo breakfast roll,
That's what he has each morning
On his way to school.

In school he gets in trouble
In class and out at play,
No lessons done, disrupting fun,
But he goes there every day.

I wonder why he bothers,
He could just stay in bed
All morning like his parents
But he doesn't. No. Instead

He rises every morning,
Walks up to the school
Knowing he'll be in trouble
When he acts the fool.

He gets up unlike the others,
I really don't know why
He comes to school each morning
But I admire this boy

Who rises undefeated
While his parents on the dole
Leave him to his cola
And a jumbo breakfast roll.

I'm Proud to be Me

Though you live in a house
With a proper address
And wear proper clothes
Not my hand-me-down dress,
Though you think that you're better
Than I'll ever be
And look down on our equals,
I'm proud to be me.

Dan Breen

For Fintan O'Toole

'There's a great gap between a gallous story and a dirty deed'

THE PLAYBOY OF THE WESTERN WORLD

My Fight for Irish Freedom by Dan Breen –
I read it like a Western; I'd pretend
To be a freedom fighter at thirteen –
It made a change from 'Cowboys'; I'd spend
My spare time freeing Ireland in my head
Reliving his adventures one by one –
The policemen that he shot at Solohead,
Romance about the days spent on the run.

A nation born of romance and of blood,
Once ruled by men who killed for their beliefs,
Now a nation grown to adulthood
Losing faith in heroes, tribal chiefs.
Dan Breen is laid with the giants who held sway;
The gallous reads of dirty deeds today.

The Mother

Forced to view his body –
Her guerrilla son
Shot dead in an ambush
By an occupier's gun;

Forced to view his body
In the workhouse where,
Lest there should be reprisals,
She could show no mother's care;

Forced to view his body,
She denied she knew her son
Then left him to an unmarked grave.
That's how the war was won.

GALVIN AND VICARS

In memoriam Mick Galvin, killed in action, Kilmorna, Knockanure (in the parish of Newtown Sandes, now Moyvane) on Thursday, 7 April, 1921; Sir Arthur Vicars, shot at Kilmorna House, his residence, on Thursday, 14 April, 1921.

Mick Galvin, Republican,
Arthur Vicars, who knows what?
– Some sort of Loyalist –
In Ireland's name were shot:

Vicars by Republicans,
Galvin by the Tans,
Both part of my history –
The parish of Newtown Sandes

Named to flatter landlords
(But 'Moyvane' today,
Though some still call it 'Newtown' –
Some things don't go away

Easily). Galvin and Vicars,
I imagine you as one –
Obverse and reverse
Sundered by the gun.

History demands
We admit each other's wrongs:
Galvin and Vicars,
Joined only in this song,

Nonetheless I join you
In the freedom of this state
For art discovers symmetries
Where politics must wait.

Tans: *i.e. Black and Tans, a unit of the Crown forces during the Irish War of Independence*

Munster Football Final 1924

Nothing polarises like a war,
And, of all wars, a civil war is worst;
It takes a century to heal the scars
And even then some names remain accursed.
The tragedies of Kerry, open wounds –
John Joe Sheehy on the run in 'twenty four,
The Munster Final in the Gaelic Grounds:
There's something more important here than war.
John Joe Sheehy, centre forward, Republican,
Con Brosnan, Free State captain, centrefield;
For what they love, they both put down the gun –
On Con's safe conduct, Sheehy takes the field.
In an hour the Kerry team will win.
Sheehy will vanish, on Brosnan's bond, again.

Ireland Takes Her Place among the Nations of the Earth

Once upon a time, I knew this place –
Everyone, their seed and generation;
Now everywhere I look, I see a face
I've never seen before, and this new nation
Is a story that has never yet been told,
A bigger story than the one we learned,
That sent men out to fight in days of old
For a vision that in hatred killed and burned.
We cannot teach that story any more
To a race as pure and white as an open page,
We welcome the new Irish at our door,
The stories that herald a new age,
The age that makes old hatreds obsolete,
The hatreds we once nursed in our defeat.

A Parent's Love

How close the sound of laughter and of tears!
My children watching Dumbo on TV
In the next room – are those wails or cheers?
At this remove their screaming worries me.

Do my children laugh or cry in the next room?
I check them out, and this is what I see –
No light illuminates the falling gloom,
Instead of watching Dumbo on TV,

High jinks on the sofa - they're both well,
I tick them off, their giggles fill and burst;
A parent's love knows all it needs of hell –
I hear them play and strangely fear the worst.

Grá Tuismitheora

Cé chomh gar 's atá glór caointe is glór gaire!
Mo pháistí ag féachaint ar Dumbo ar TV
Sa seomra suite taobh liom, i dtús báire
Ní aithním an bhfuilid ag gol nó ag gáirí.

Ag gáirí nó ag gol sa seomra suite?
Téim isteach, táid ag déanamh spraoi
Ar an dtolg is oíche beagnach tite;
In ionad a bheith ag féachaint ar TV,

High jinks ar an dtolg, ní baol dóibh,
Mé ag tabhairt amach, iadsan ag sciotaíl,
Leanann a Ifreann féin grá an tuismitheora –
Agus iad ag gáirí, is eagal liom iad i mbaol.

To My Son as He Leaves Home

Son, just to have you 'round the house is good,
The way you make your presence felt. I'll miss
The way that being with you was drink and food;
The future beckons, now it's come to this.
You're leaving, son, I wish you all the best,
May every good that life can give be yours,
Stand firm, love, when life becomes a test,
Remember that the good you do endures.
You're leaving, son, take all you need from me,
It's freely given as it was when you
Needed me, a baby on my knee,
Needed me as to a man you grew.
I love you son, I shed a happy tear
As I let you go in faith and hope and fear.

To My Daughter, Pregnant

She brings me eggs from chickens she has reared,
Cabbages and carrots she has grown,
All the things about her for which I feared
Have come to naught: she's come into her own.
She brings me eggs from chickens she has reared,
Soon she'll be a mother. I rejoice.
Daughter, from the moment you appeared,
You gave me songs to sing in joyful voice.
Soon you'll be a mother and you'll give
Not eggs just, but a grandchild to adore,
Another reason for a man to live
For a grandchild adds its blessings to our store.
Pregnant with the life in which you bloom,
You bless us with the child within your womb.

Nanas

Nanas give you goodies
When mammies say they can't
'Cos Nanas always give you
Exactly what you want
And mammies can't give out to them
'Cos they are very old
And that's why they're allowed to be
Very, very bold.

Sonnet to Brenda

I won't compare you to a summer's day,
The beaches all deserted in the rain –
Some way, this, to spend a holiday
(You're sorry now you didn't book for Spain).
No! The weather can't be trusted in these parts –
It's fickle as a false love's said to be;
I could get sentimental about hearts
But that's not my style. Poetry,
The only thing that's constant in my life,
The only thing I know that still is true
As my love remains for you, dear wife –
This, then, is what I'll compare to you.
The iambic heart that pulses in these lines
Measures out my love. And it still rhymes.

Just to be Beside You is Enough

Just to be beside you is enough,
Just to make your breakfast tea and toast,
To help you with the ware, that kind of stuff,
Just to get the papers and your post;
To hold you in my arms in calm embrace,
Just to sit beside you at the fire,
Just to trace my fingers on your face
Is more to me than all of youth's desire;
Just to lie beside you in the night,
To hear you breathe in peace before I sleep,
To wake beside you in the morning light
In the love we sowed together that we reap.
Together we have taken smooth and rough.
Just to be beside you is enough.

Old Lovers

To Brenda on our Fortieth Wedding Anniversary

This is how it is between old lovers,
A peck upon the lips is all they need
Where once was youthful lust between bedcovers
(How closely youthful lust resembles greed);
This is how it is between old lovers,
Lifelong friends together holding hands,
Together there's a peace that they discover,
The kind old lovers truly understand;
This is how it is between old lovers,
Shopping with their grandchildren for toys
All that age has lost they now recover,
The jaded world returned to surprise
For this is how it is between old lovers,
Life reserves for them its greatest joys.

Reading William Wordsworth

'Oh joy! that in our embers …' Come off it, head!
Just because you're past it doesn't mean
The rest of us must join the living dead;
My youth long past, I still am full of beans.
'Oh joy! that in our embers …' Get a life!
Like one whose heart is fresh and full of dreams,
Delighting in my children, grandkids, wife,
I'm happier now than I have ever been.
Examined, life's worth living. How much time
I've left here doesn't bother me at all.
My course complete, resolved at last in rhyme,
I sing, oh joy! being still on fire, enthralled.
So raise your glass and join me in my song,
Drink to life! Stop moping! And move on!

Drinking in the Square

The Small Square, Listowel, Autumn 2023

Earth has not anything to show more fair
It seems to me this morning over coffee in the Square,
'The Left Bank' I call it, that's what it is to me
Beside the bookshops, the artist's, and the statue of John B.

People passing by me, stopping for a chat,
Wake me from my reverie; they get what I'm at,
Locals who know their poetry and art,
For the poet and the artist an audience apart.

Beneath these trees that shade me as I sit here in the Square
I think of William Wordsworth and the London he thought fair
But I wouldn't swap my 'Left Bank' for his London's mighty heart,
For where I am this morning turning life to art.

Acknowledgements

Acknowledgements are due to the following publishers, where all but the uncollected poems listed below were published: Arlen House, Beaver Row Press, Cló Iar Chonnacht, Coiscéim, Liberties Press, Marino Books, Mercier Press, Peterloo Poets (UK), Poolbeg Press, Revival Press, Salmon Poetry, Story Line Press (US) and Wolfhound Press.

Many thanks to the following where the uncollected poems were first published: *The Irish Times:* 'Old Lovers'; *Quadrant* (Australia): 'Reading William Wordsworth'; *The Kerryman:* 'Drinking in the Square'.

Thanks also to *Sunday Miscellany,* RTÉ Radio 1 for broadcasting the uncollected 'I Sing of Michael Hartnett'.

The Quiet Quarter, Lyric fm for broadcasting the uncollected 'Ireland Takes her Place among the Nations of the Earth'.

Biographical Note

Gabriel Fitzmaurice was born, in 1952, in the village of Moyvane, Co. Kerry where he still lives. For over thirty years he taught in the local primary school from which he retired as principal in 2007. He is author of more than sixty books, including collections of poetry in English and Irish as well as several collections of verse for children. He has translated extensively from the Irish and has edited a number of anthologies of poetry in English and Irish. He has published volumes of essays and collections of songs and ballads. Poems of his have been set to music and recorded by Brian Kennedy and performed by the RTÉ Cór na nÓg with the RTÉ National Symphony Orchestra. An Honorary Member of the Széchenyi Academy of Letters and Arts in Hungary, he is a recipient of the Listowel Writers' Week John B. Keane Lifetime Achievement Award. He frequently broadcasts on radio and television on culture and the arts.

www.ingramcontent.com/pod-product-compliance
Lightning Source LLC
LaVergne TN
LVHW041634070426
835507LV00008B/619